Yield To The Genius Within

You Can Make
Something Significant Out of Your Life

Ken Little

DOORWAY
Publications

Published by D O O R W A Y Publications
by www.AmazingInternationalPublishing.com

Printed in the United States of America
ISBN   978-1-876022-00-6

First Edition

Special Acknowledgement
By Ken Little

For The Valuable Contribution
of Patty Little

The bride of my youth and the love of my life,
Patty Little, has contributed in a major way to
The development of
Yield to The Genius Within from the outset.
She refined the ideas and edited the
manuscript .
Thanks for Your Valuable Contribution Patty

Read On & You Will Discover
Success Belongs To You

Table of Contents

Introduction - Setting The Scene

You need to know that what you read here comes from the 'school' of hard knocks. My school has been a life as a teacher and a small business owner.

My reason for writing this book is to motivate you to avoid the outcome I gained after faithfully serving my last employer for 12 years. Budget cuts meant my services were no longer needed.

This forced me to Yield to The Genius Within.

My hope is you'll choose to Yield to The Genius Within so you can take control of your future. And so you'll never lose another night's sleep worrying about how to survive when your services are no longer needed.

Take heart, when you do Yield to The Genius Within you'll discover the best is yet to come.

Contact
Ken Little Can Be Contacted at his blog –

www.YieldToTheGeniusWithin.com/blog1
Click the Contact link and fill in your details.

You Can Make
Something Beautiful
Out of Your Life –
As You Choose To Change

"Your task is to "unearth"
this one product
which has been buried
under years of school education.
Your reward -
being changed into the person
everyone seeks out … "

Chapter 1
Success Belongs To You

So Exactly What Is The Genius Within?
It is a God given talent or ability you receive at birth. It has been defined as an -

- Activity in Life You're Best at In Your City

- Activity Where you say "I'm Born To Be This"

- Activity Where You Say "I'm Totally Fulfilled"

- Activity Hook of Those Craving Your Services

- Activity Where Time Seems To Stop Still

Your Journey Begins
You began life in a special race and you won. Your race was against more than 5 million other sperm and you were racing to claim the right to become a human being.

Congratulations on winning the race of a lifetime. The good news continues. This was a great event for more than one reason. You see the truth is you were born a genius.

Yes you. The gift of God for you at birth was the ability to do one thing better than anyone else. You heard that right. There is one product or service that you were born to provide for your community at a level of excellence no other human can come near.

Your task is to "unearth" this one product as you commit to your new "changing my life" program. Remember this one product has been buried under years of probably necessary but sometimes tedious school education.

Your reward will be being changed into the person that everyone seeks out. They will be keen to buy your products and services.

Genius Secrets Partly Revealed

For you to get the most out of your Genius Within we need to take a closer look at some definitions of the word "genius".

Here are a few that you may discover are helpful-
1. **Someone** who has exceptional ability and originality

2. **Ace**: someone who is dazzlingly skilled in an area maybe just gaining recognition or popularity

3. **Flair**: a natural talent; "she has a flair for decorating" or "cooking"

You will have heard of people with "exceptional ability" and of those who are an "ace" in their chosen field.. What you may well not know is how they got the recognition for their creative gift.

They got it because they were willing to yield to their Genius in an economic meltdown. Necessity was the mother of invention. Suddenly they found their customer group greatly reduced in number.

In these times of economic uncertainty it's critical that you, as a business owner accept that the customer of yesterday is gone. You also need to know that to get the new customer to buy you have to reinvent yourself in a manner yet to be tried.

You must dig deep to get more from your performance as a marketer, The Genius Within needs to be your best friend as you consider your options for " changing my life ".

How To Yield To Your Genius

You are probably asking yourself how you Yield to Your Genius. The best answer to that question comes from taking a look at dictionary meanings of "yield". These include -

- full surrender
- give up oneself to an inclination
- give up-cease resistance to someone

Your Genius self longs for you to surrender to him and to stop resisting attempts to bless you by taking complete control of your life. He wants other people to see you as the gifted person you really are, with special products and services to offer.

The best way to surrender is to give up control of your life in key areas. Begin with your thought life. Instead of pushing aside the next creative thought embrace it, write it down and own it. Then move on to your feelings.

The next time you feel you've got more talent than the undervalued person you're treated as by family and friends, thank God that you really are as special as you think.

Take a lesson from Joseph in the Old Testament. He shared with family he was going to be a leader. They mocked and shunned him.

Finally, watch your actions. For example, you may behave like an average baseball player, but deep inside you know you're going to be a champ.

Start acting like the champ you know you can be. In particular start talking like the champ. The champ is the Genius Within.   He wants you to ask yourself "How should I be changing my life ?"

Benefits from Your Yield to the Genius

Your benefits begin with the ability to offer a service or product which cannot be matched by anyone else, even in these challenging times of economic meltdown. This provides permission to charge a premium price for a superior product.

You will be blessed in more ways than one as you yield to your Genius Within. Just as you are you will be empowered to be a significant blessing to others.

Bill Gates has yielded to his genius and has given himself and his wife the freedom to transform the lives of thousands of less fortunate people in Africa, through the charity work of the Bill and Melinda Gates Foundation. $67 billion and growing has been contributed since they yielded to the genius.

You need to know that the amount of anyone's contribution to the less fortunate of the world is not the key issue. The key is the genuine intent anyone expresses to assisting a change close to their heart. That assistance will be given when you send a clear message –"I'm changing my life"

At a personal level you will benefit from yielding to your Genius as you assist family to meet pressing financial needs. They will start saying "she's changing my life."

A Special Kind of Genius –
The Footpath Library Lady

Sarah owns a Video Production company. Her kind of genius comes under definition one – an exceptional ability. It's an ability of the heart. With this ability to love street people in her city she began to hand out free books nightly in 2003.

Others were feeding their need for food. She wanted to give them mind and heart food. Starting the Footpath Library in 2003 with an old car, used books and a big heart, her service has spread to other cities and now enjoys solid community support. Sarah has been recognized by the community not for her IQ, but for her HQ – her Heart Quotient.

She has given significance and dignity back to the lives of many homeless folk. Michael was one such person. Forced to live on the street by tragic events this former artist has returned to a well funded creative work life and has had his work regularly exhibited in the State Gallery.

Sarah was responding to the death of a young friend and had a strong desire to help others less fortunate. She can teach us many lessons about the importance of coming to a point of deciding to Yield to The Genius Within.

Perhaps the key lesson is that yielding is not always an intentional act but a flow-on impact to you loving someone so much that you devote your life's work to putting right a wrong that was done.

In Sarah's case she felt deeply that what she had observed society doing to the newly homeless man was wrong. She also believes she is correcting that wrong by starting the Footpath Library to provide much needed 'food" for the mind of the homeless city dwellers. This was her answer to the question "How should I be changing my life to help others?"

She has learned that her Giving Work has been an important part of her plan to Yield To The Genius Within. Her Giving Work has directly impacted her success as a marketer of her Video Production service.

Your Giving Work will also impact your success as a marketer.

**You Can Make
Something Beautiful
Out of Your Life –
As You Choose
To Embrace Change**

"The world is changing fast.
One of the best ways to
get the best out of yourself is
to start a new line…"

Chapter 2
You Can Discover
Your Genius

Why Yield To The Genius Within?
Because You Need..……... (The Outline)

- To Find Career in Small Business

- To Build a New Business

- To Dig Deeper

- New Learning for Earning Options

- To Get the Best Out of Yourself

- To Do More With Less Cash

- To Be Significant in The New Discoveries

- Client Reconnection- Yesterday's Client Gone

Why Yield To The Genius Within?
Because You Need...... (The Details)
1. To Find a Career in Small Business

You've lost your job or expect to lose one soon and want a new one to enable you to keep on paying the bills.   Success Belongs To You when it comes to starting a new business because The Genius Within can help you find a hungry market, and Say "I'm changing my life to get my finances back in order"

2. To Build a New Business

Your business has collapsed and you need to find another to maintain your lifestyle. These are desperate times we live in and they require desperate measures. To get the answers you need to pull through you need to ask the right questions.

When you Yield to the Genius it's easier to discover what these questions are. Questions like "What else should I be doing in changing my life?"

3. To Dig Deeper

Because you've reached rock bottom and you need to "dig" deeper. Experience has shown the best place to start to "dig" deeper is within yourself. Down on the inside you've got resources which you've never found because you've never needed them - now you do. Seek and you'll find.

4. New Learning for Earning Options

You urgently need new education options as the system has stopped working for you and your family. Self- directed learning is the way of the future. Getting this done will require you to yield to The Genius.

5. To Get the Best Out of Yourself

The world is changing fast. One of the best ways to get the best out of yourself is to start a new line in your own business after you Yield to The Genius Within.

6. To Do More With Less Cash

Now you're having to wrestle with financial challenges with new urgency. You' need to find new ways to stretch your budget dollar. You are ready to yield to the cash saving Genius Within as you ask yourself "In what other ways could I be changing my life financially?"

7. To Be Significant in The New Discoveries

You are living in the midst of waves of new discoveries. They range from devices to make the use of home ladders safer, to complex processes to take us to the next level beyond digital technology.

You need to be willing to have an offline operation together with your online one.

Many non professionals are inventing for the first time. You could be one of them. Yield to the creative genius within.

Hot areas include alternative fuels and lifestyle patterns (many people living to 100). You can be sure they're saying "How can I be changing my life to help myself?"

You could discover your true significance and gain recognition much more easily as you actively seek for opportunities to meet the new needs emerging in your community.

8. Client Reconnection

Yes, the client of yesterday has gone. As a marketer you need to relearn what's involved in the buying decision.

The team at Hyundai have gone through this change. They now take back the new car you bought if you lose your job in the year after purchase.

The result has been an increase of 1,000's in new vehicle sales and only a handful of returns.

Innovative solutions are able to be generated in teams more easily when you first Yield to the Genius. Two heads really are better than one.

You need new ways to regain lost customers by saying daily "I'm changing my life and sales techniques to help out customers?"

Give them the certainty they crave in economic meltdown mode by offering to assist them to meet their needs long term at low or no cost.

As a marketer of information products, you could offer them all your products for the next 12 months for the price you'd normally charge for one. That gets their attention and ensures lifelong customer loyalty.

You Can Make
Something Beautiful
Out of Your Life –
As You Choose
To Love Change

"Impartation Secret–
Gaining
Your Mentor's Lifestyle"

Chapter 3
Whatsoever
You Can Believe

Your Genius Understands What to Read

You can begin to discover your Genius by being prepared to learn how your Genius Learns. You'll find it easy and interesting.

The truth is only your Genius Within knows how to Power Read. Your Genius also understands what to read, but we will get to that a little later. First, let's go into the "how to" concerning your daily reading experience.

Levels of Acceptance and Your Genius

You see you read with one Level of Acceptance and your Genius reads at 8 Levels. You can learn how that's done as easily as you learned the ABC in grade school when education was more formal.

A little earlier you read "Your Genius also understands what to read". What he reads falls into the Written Word and the World Around Us. The first area–the Written Word includes The Word of God, The Bible, and the Words in All Other Books.

We are concerned in this book with the Words in All Other Books and the idea that you are at the moment only a Level 1 reader. You are missing so much.

The reason why we are so concerned with this here is that the meltdown has meant you need to improve your performance even to hold markets you're in. Reading with the best Level of Acceptance gives your performance a great boost and builds your business's bottom line monthly performance.

Two of the benefits of embracing the Levels of Acceptance idea are as follows. First, it will turn every book purchase into a highly profitable investment in your "changing my life" program.

Secondly, it will give you, the Power Reader, the lifestyle of the author. History abounds with stories of people who have had this exciting and achievable experience.

Reading the World Around Us

Now, let's go a little deeper on the second area mentioned above – The World Around Us. The people watcher in you is constantly "reading" the world around you to discover things new and exciting.

The process of discovering your Genius requires an increased level of awareness of the person hidden within.- the true you. To maintain a correct balance in your life you need to develop increased awareness of the people surrounding your daily life.

You need to know this increased level of awareness can be brought about by a choice you make or by force of circumstances. Such circumstances are often formed by the valley floor experiences of losing a loved one or a livelihood.

A Key Factor to Discovering
Your Genius Within

An old time preacher shares how much control we have over our circumstances. He tells us you can't stop the "crows" flying over our lives but you sure can stop them nesting in your hair. The "crows" were life's challenges that everyone faced daily.

.

A modern translation is that we can't prevent some challenges but we can prevent them having a lasting impact by what we think of ourselves after the event. When we choose to think more of ourselves we say "I'm changing my life" in such a way that every passing circumstances builds long term strength."

The Secret is - It Says Heart Not Head

You may have heard- "As a man thinks in his heart so is he" There is a secret in this saying that you are going to learn and, if you let it, it will change your life.

The secret is discovered by recognizing, as I've done after 29 years of research, that most read the above expression as-
"As a man thinks in his HEAD so is he". The fact is it says HEART not head. This makes a big difference.

Before we go further on this exciting journey you need to know what your "Heart" is not. It's not the organ in your chest that pumps blood for you.

A good demonstration of what the "Heart" is, is found on programs like Britain's Got Talent. In the interviews before they go on stage contestants reveal a lot. You will recall seeing some who, when asked if they think they can win, will say in a head response, "Yes" and think it would be nice.

In contrast, other contestants, asked the same question, give a Heart response "Yes" and share they have a deep inner knowing they will win.

The difference between the first and second type of contestants is that only the second type really believes deep inside themselves that success belongs to them. Only this group know the truth behind -"As a man thinks in his heart so is he"- and their successful outcomes show it. The good news for you is that with a little practice you can become one who "thinks in his heart...".

Ladies, please don't be put off by the use of "man". It's used in the sense of mankind so you are included.   There is no doubt you can be whatever you think you are but only if you do your thinking in your heart not your head. For you to receive this properly you need to be open minded, then you can improve, with practice.

You've got more than one mind, a Heart Mind and a Head Mind - both have to be committed to your "changing my life" program.

Impartation Secret–
Gaining Your Mentor's Lifestyle

Your plan to Yield to The Genius Within is made much easier when you get hold of The Impartation Secret.

This works best when you're not completely sure about the nature of Your Genius but you do have a mentor you long to be like.   There is only space to give one example of this here but you'll get the idea I'm sure. Study this twice and learn. Sam (real names not used here for privacy reasons) worked for the government but his heart's desire was to be a motivational speaker just like Brian his mentor.

Brian was famous and traveled widely across all states. Sam was unable to follow him due to his day job so he decided to purchase one of Brian's videos to do an in-depth study of his style of presentation. He watched the video 123 times and began offering his services as a motivational speaker at lunch club meetings for free.

He continued this as his skills developed. He loved what he did but still had to keep the day job. The audiences loved him, so much so that they commented to Brian's office that there was a new guy doing the speaker circuit who sounded just like him.

Brian and his managers came along to one of the lunch meetings and discovered , with eyes closed, it was not possible to tell the difference in sound between Sam and Brian. Also their presentation styles were identical. He said "I've worked hard at "changing my life"

Sam got an invitation to join Brian on the road for a few seminars and gained so much promotion he was able to start out on his own. He went on to live the lifestyle of his famous mentor.

He knew the secret to his success was watching the Brian video repeatedly, so many times.

You could have the same success as Sam, should it be your heart's desire to do so, just by getting an impartation of your mentor's talent by watching a DVD – at least 123 times. Repetition is the key.

**You Can Make
Something Beautiful
Out of Your Life –
As You Choose
To Get Change First**

"Get The Messenger
Before You Get The Message"

Chapter 4
The Power of Life & Death

Naming Rights over Your Life

In the tongue rests the power of life and death. You will be aware of the power a judge has in states where capital punishment is still practiced. The judge has the authority to impose a death sentence on a convicted felon.

Your authority is far greater. You can speak your heart's desire over your life's work and your business. A story my grandmother told me highlights this power and authority.

She lived in the Bahamas. As a local she enjoyed trips over to her favorite place – Hog Island. The water was always crystal clear and it was the most beautiful place on God's earth.

All the locals loved it but few tourists were interested in visiting a place called Hog Island. It's name brought to mind a picture of a place populated by wild hogs.

Hog Island was one of the locals' best kept secrets. Out of the blue a real estate developer came along and bought up an estate in liquidation due to no land buyers.

To boost sales he thought he'd change the name of the place. He was not sure this was a "changing my life" experience but he wanted to try it.

He completed the paperwork to have the name changed from Hog Island to Paradise Island. The rest, as they say, is history. Paradise Island soon became the winter home of the rich.

Because the Developer Changed the Name
Just because the developer changed the name to Paradise Island confirms you can speak your heart's desire over your life.

That simple act may well bring out The Genius and give you the major breakthrough you've been intensely desiring.

Whilst you may not have had a grandmother who lived in the Bahamas, you'll probably have lived in or traveled through a city filled with skyscrapers.

They have a major tenant and only that tenant has naming rights over the building.

They legally have the power, influence and authority to determine all matters related to the use and operation of the floor space they occupy.

Crossing over from buildings to people there is evidence of the Paradise Principle.

In an inauguration ceremony the peoples' electoral choice officially becomes The President of the United States of America. He's changed for life.

Closer to home actors and actresses cast aside their common name to take on a screen name.
Would Rock Hudson have gained fame without this screen name?

Does that simple change of name bring fame and fortune?   You could prove this for yourself. This is a serious step.

It should only be taken on the advice of professional advisers, as you ask "How can I be changing my life to benefit me in future years?".

I've had clients who were sexual abuse victims who've done it. They got set free from a life of guilt and defeat.

The outcome is not necessarily fame and fortune but it sure is new life for them. And they got closure from their victim experience in the old life.

In that new life The Genius Within has the opportunity to emerge.

How often have you seen others find their life significance by coming out of a time of suffering and giving themselves to helping others?

The Genius Within is often sparked by encounters like this or the suffering experiences of others. The good news is a thriving community based business has often been founded on removing these experiences from people's lives.

Get The Messenger Before You Get The Message
By now you see words have a big impact on your life and the way your business unfolds. We rely on books, ebooks and other documents to give us the information we need.

You are most likely not aware of it but you're not getting the quality of information you need because you have failed to check one of the most basic assumptions.

It's the assumption you're reading correctly and getting all you could from the books you read. Truth is you are not. The good news is that you are able to fix it.

The Genius Within You knows correct reading requires you "get" the messenger before you "get" the message.

37 years of studying the process of reading has shown me that behind all we read in every book – which I view as The Message – is the Messenger.

Look carefully at the next book you are reading and you'll see him as more than the author.

Here is one key lesson I've learned. If you come to a time of reading a book with the wrong attitude you've just wasted your time.

If on the inside you're saying, "I'm on the look out to find fault with your ideas so prove yourself to me", you will gain no "changing my life" experience from the read.

On the other hand you will gain the most if, before you start reading, you temporarily suspend all disbelief on the subject and distrust of the author.

You must come with an open mind and, most importantly, an open heart to the author. The key is the Intent you have in your heart as you take the author's work in your hands.

"Get" acquainted with the author. Treat them like a friend. Only then will they share their full ideas with you.

You see reading a book is so much more than getting eye contact with the text on the pages. It's all about getting Heart Contact with the messenger and author so the content on the pages will flood into your life.

It will come in such a way that it has the power to give you the breakthroughs in life you are seeking.

So, next time you open a book be sure to "Get" Heart Contact with The Messenger Before You Get The Message.

.

You Can Make
Something Beautiful
Out of Your Life –
As You Choose
To Value LifeStory Change

"Your Life Story Has Many
Hidden Riches for Readers"

Chapter 5
Hidden Riches
- Secret Places

Discovering & Processing Internal Riches
Into External Riches

Your future financial security, in this time of economic meltdown, depends on you finding and making money out of Hidden Riches. You will be pleased to discover secret places containing your hidden riches can be found without the need for airline tickets. Your "changing my life" program will get a boost here.

In fact some of the most valuable Hidden Riches can be found deep in your heart. Before we highlight some of them it will help you if I explain the process we are going to use. We are seeking to discover riches which are Internal to your life to assist you to make External riches, using principles which are Eternal. What do we mean by that?

Internal riches are the experiences you have hidden in the depths of your heart which can be "dug up" and brought to light to add value to your life and dollars to your bank balance.

Harnessing Eternal Principles- Create External Riches

Eternal principles are those in the Bible. These can be used by both believers and unbelievers. The principles include "Seek and you shall find" together with "Occupy until I come".

Would you like an example of these in action? I thought so. OK, consider the experience of Joshua" who recently lost his middle management job

He had done much seeking for a new position without success. He decided to "Occupy" by doing what he hadn't done since he was a kid. He was intent on getting his "changing my life" program.

He dug up his front lawn and planted a vegetable garden. You're going to be seeing a lot of these sprouting up in the future but that's a subject for another book. As he dug he recalled the pleasant times spent as a boy learning organic gardening and companion planting.

Joshua lived in a settled area in the midst of retirees keen to do no more than watch TV all day.

"Starving" New Clients Are
Closer Than You Think

Neighbors walked by and saw the contentment on his face as he tended his cabbages and tomatoes. They wanted to chat about the conversion of his manicured lawn into a colorful vegetable garden. As his work thrived his reputation grew. Others called on him to produce a bountiful garden.

They were happy to pay him for his services as they knew they would gain the great feeling of having passers by admire their new gardens - just as they had admired his.

In a short time this former manager had established not only a thriving organic garden but also a business as an organic gardening consultant.

Your Life Story-Hidden Riches for Readers

You need to realize and make money out of the fact, in your life you have solved problems others are still desperate to solve..

And you found ways to find more profitable businesses. You've been asking What can I do toward "changing my life"?

You've done a lot of different things in your travels, and seen the many unusual ways people make a living. There are many future clients out there who would gladly pay you well to learn of your discoveries, solutions and innovative ideas.

- Ideas for Starting a New High Profit Business
- Tips for a Better Job or Higher Yield Business
- A Breakthrough to Return a Business to Profit

Hear Stories from Strangers - Start a JV

You might like to give thought to this story and consider how the Yield to the Genius Within process worked. Get ready to be surprised how simple but powerful the steps were.

This is a true story and it could be just as easily be your story if you had taken time to Yield to the Genius Within by being prepared to take the time to actively listen to stories told by strangers.

I call this The Stranger Monetization Formula.

At a local Coffee Club, Jim, was telling Mario, a great story.. Jim shared he'd come from remote Cambodia where he saw an amazing sight. He spotted cows eating what he knew were cashew bushes. When he asked the village farmer what they were eating, the reply was "weeds".

He told Carlo he knew nothing about the cashew industry and said it was a shame nothing could be done with these "weeds". Mario laughed. Jim asked what was funny. Mario shared he can't believe this news.. You see, He's a nut importer. He imports 200 tons of cashews a year, from high priced sources. Retail value of this market…..

"Weeds" Worth $4million Each Year

Jim returned to Cambodia, with Mario's help, to set up a joint venture with the farmers. The farmers, Jim, and Carlo, all get a fair share from the sale of these "weeds" worth $4million each year.

Could you have such a Story Sharing experience at your local coffee shop? Yes you can. If you Yield To The Genius Within.   Have respect for strangers. Taking this action gives you connections you need to do the greatest good in this world.

Your Genius Revealed in Your Life Story
Learn to Value Your Story As You Should
You may be surprised, after reading the above Story Sharing, to find one of your most valuable hidden riches is your life story.

37 years of consulting with clients has proved this to me many times.

Keep reading and you'll discover 3 good Benefits for creating your life story and knowing "I'm changing my life "

We tend to place little value on the routine experiences that make up our life story because we think they would be of no interest to others.   The truth is people love stories, particularly if they involve you overcoming challenges.

Not a writer? - DO NOT PANIC – Read on.
If, like many people you freeze at the thought of writing anything, let alone your life story, relax because I'm going to show you an easy way to do this with none of the hassles of using a keyboard.

Around your home you'll have an old cassette recorder or an mp3 recorder.

Use these to record your life story in short parts, have a friend write it out for you, and your fears of writing will disappear. Now here are the 3 benefits I promised to share with you earlier.

Benefit 1
As You Share You Unlock More Memories
You will find the more you share of your story the more memories will be unlocked. Memories that others value - memories that make you money in hard times.

Benefit 2
As You Share Your Victories Others Flow
Telling the stories of your victories gives listeners the strength to believe they too can overcome the challenges.

Benefit 3
Record the Story to Shape Future Goals
One of the most powerful benefits from recording your life story is that it gives you a list of past experiences you can use to prepare goals to shape your future.

Beyond these three, your greatest benefit is you're following a direction to Yield to TheGenius. You're also working your "changing my life" program.

You Can Make Something Beautiful Out of Your Life – As You Choose To Change Your Thinking

"Idea Farming – Harvesting Your Genius Fruit"

Chapter 6
Putting Your Genius
to Work

Your Exciting Journey's Key Steps

Think, Link, Ink are Key Steps in your journey to put Your Genius to work for you. You'll find this an exciting journey because you are about to learn more about yourself than you've ever known before.

As a Yield To The Genius Consultant for 37 years I've some powerful secrets I'd like to share.

The Key Steps to
Think, Link, Ink Can Be Used by You

All It Takes is Time, Patience and Repetition
Your Thoughts Contain Money Makers
Get Still & Think-Link-Ink- Your Genius Pops Out.

What are the Key Steps to Think Link, Ink?

Good question. To begin with, Think requires you to use your little gray cells and have a high regard for what they are producing.

Tell yourself you're a special kind of Einstein- because you are. Take a lead from your role model Albert. He said imagination was more important than knowledge.

So use plenty of Imagination when you are thinking. You will discover it boosts your business.

Think also requires you focus on remembering what is important. Albert, when he was developing his Theory of Relativity, would go for an evening walk. Each time he set out from home he had to take with him a scrap of paper with his address on it as he was unable to remember it. Though, he never forgot his Theory of Relativity.

Make Your Link Every Time

Link requires you to use your imagination to link together what seem to be unrelated and undervalued thoughts.

This process is used by consulting giants, like Jay Abraham and Tony Robbins, and with practice you can change your life.

When you Yield to the Genius Within you will automatically make the Link each time. You will get a clearer picture of this process if I share a recent example from my own business. I was looking for new areas of data on customer preferences to meet those needs in a more targeted way with my product offers.

As the Think step in the process I considered a source most others place no marketing value on – the comments under YouTube videos. In the Link step, I found plenty that told me why consumers wanted their products of choice.

Intense In-Depth Self Interviewing

Now, in the Ink step of the process, things get a little more technical. Ink simply put means getting your discoveries down on paper.

That's right just with pen and paper you record all your findings in what I call Intense In-Depth Self Interviewing.

Due to lack of space here I can only tell you it involves putting all my feelings thoughts words and actions, on a given event, under a special kind of "microscope" It's very powerful.

Summary Steps-Putting TheGenius to Work

You can begin tonight. You'll find your most creative thoughts come in the night. That's because you experience too much "interference" in the day.

It's important to capture all these "seeds". Have a notepad and pen by your bed. Be prepared to wake and write down all thoughts.

Don't give any thought to them being good or useless. Just put them down. From the first time you do this you will feel so good you'll be won over to this new habit.

Idea Farming – Harvesting Your Genius Fruit - Think

Seed -   First Thought – Capture in Notepad

Seedling -   Baby Thought-Wait–"Water It"

Small Bush–   Kid Thought "Fertilize It" "Prune It"

Full Tree –   Adult Thought" "Harvest It"

Link
Connecting the Seemingly Unconnected

Building Money Bridges Between Them

Ink – Get The Thoughts Into Print
Write – Record – Thoughts at Each Stage

Level 1 Review – Inspect Words, Themes, Niches

Level 2 Review – Detect Monetizable Niches

Level 3 Review – Niche Selection for Products

I hope you find this process useful . I've used it with success for 19 years.

Further Gems- Use in Your Ongoing Learning
Here are three more discoveries I've made. I know they'll be a blessing to you on your learning for earning journey.

- You Learn Uniquely Compared to Others
- Knowing How You Learn is a Key
- Who You Learn With Shapes Your Outcomes

You can use these for great personal gain – as long as the reason you desire the gain is to give you the ability to leave the world a better place.

You Can Make
Something Beautiful
Out of Your Life –
As You Choose
To Change Your Feelings

"You Can & You Should
Yield To The Genius Within"

Chapter 7
You Were Born a Winner

Gather Up The Fragments That Remain
& Be Blessed

You get a special reward for reading Yield to The Genius Within this far. The reason you get it is because a main message of this book is to finish what you start, including the reading of all books. The truth is you need to read this book at least three times to get a full measure of the message.

Each time you read you will gather fragments of information you missed on earlier reads. One of your special rewards is you learn of recent lessons I've learned in my own journey as I Yield to The Genius Within. The first lesson is that there is a vast area of new opportunity opening up for alert entrepreneurs.

You Can Profit From Recent Lessons

You will have seen news items concerning people living longer. At present many are reaching 115. Japan now has 32,000 citizens who are 100 years or more. That's a trend being found in many countries.

I have it on good authority, The Bible, people will start living to 120. This will create opportunities like never before. Some of the more obvious ones are-

- Gardening Businesses for 60 Plus Market
- Government Contracts to Get 60+ Back to Work
- Insurance Start Ups - Premiums Paid to 100
- Training Programs for the 80 Plus Folk
- Travel Groups for the Super Seniors

This is a small selection of the opportunities that are opening up. There will be many more. You can see the potential in the above areas but none of them covers the biggest area of need for those who are babyboomers and older.

Profit From This Secret Need in Your City

In my Yield to The Genius walk I've begun talking to others who are 60 Plus about the issues surrounding what they call "Refirement". They have no interest in the usual retirement subjects of retirement villages, nursing homes or talking about their latest knee replacement.

At first their key challenge seems to be that they suffer from a deep loneliness. Probing brings out a longing to be significant in the community- in an area different to their working life.

You can meet this need in your city but don't dare suggest they do volunteer work. An actor, 80, in my city asked on TV why he was seeking work explained perfectly "I need the money". Another wanted to keep making a contribution to society.

A lot of mature folk give me the same messages. It seems to be because, when they entered the work force, people retired at 65 and had expired before they were 66. But now they have already survived an extra 14 years and they figure they could go to 100. And many will. Social security systems will fail and pension funds will run out because of that.

Will you allow your walk to Yield to include adding significance to the lives of this group? As you meet their needs, yours will be met . I hope you find this information useful in getting set up.

Harnessing The Winner In You - Be A Winner
You were born a Winner because The Genius is Within you. A key part to your plan to Yield to The Genius Within is to be the winner you were meant to be. Keep in mind it's The Genius who gives you the power to excel in your chosen area.

You may be a Genius affiliate marketer or a great golfer. Know this, in your area of excellent performance you should learn to give The Genius the time he needs to grow inside you. Know what it is you yearn to spend your life excelling at.

Know How You Learn- Perfect How You Earn

Know how you learn. Schools hammer what you learn is key. How you learn is more important.

When you get the Yearning and Learning stages perfected the Earning stage will get much easier. Knowing who you are as a Learner can show you exactly what you want out of life.

Once you know What it is then the How to get it steps are made plain to you. Think like a Winner, Feel like a Winner, Speak like a Winner and you will Be a Winner.

Do The Winning

Because you were born a Winner who has decided to commit to BE a Winner you'll find it a lot easier to DO the Winning.

As you set your heart to being a winner learn how to fail your way to success. Failure events don't make you a failure. They're mileposts on the road to your next mountain top experience.

Giving Back From The Winner In You

A big part of your success, from your Yield to the Genius , comes from sharing your experience. You do this by speaking publicly on the subject.

When you heed the call to your Genius Within you need to let the members of social network communities know what you've discovered about yourself. You share any talent you're developing into a business.

Can The Disabled Yield To The Genius?

You may be surprised to learn this is a question close to my heart and whilst there is not space to explain why, the answer is a definite YES.

In fact, I believe the so called "disabled" are more accurately referred to as the Otherwise Abled because they can do things you and I can not.

My best example to confirm they can Yield To The Genius Within is a young motivational speaker named Nick Vujicic, he is so full of life.

Others view him as severely disabled. Nick was born with no arms , no legs and his proclamation is-
"No arms, no legs, no worries"

Nick has heeded the call to Yield to the Genius Within. He has been on The Hour of Power and he inspires people wherever he speaks.

You can go to YouTube.com and search for a video "Nick Vujicic". To make sure you get the right video with the high School audience here's the exact web address. Just type this into your Internet web browser -
http://www.youtube.com/watch?v=v4uG2kSdd- 4&feature=related

Watch this video and take a look at the High School kids faces. I see first a look of amazement and then a dawning realization if he can conquer challenges then they can too.

Making Best Use of What You've Got
As Nick has no arms to wave and no feet to dance with he has to make best use of his voice, his eyes, and his smile. You will see from the video he does a great job of making best use of what he's got.

You will learn powerful business building lessons as you consider how much Nick must have come to love himself to be able to stand before thousands and say – "I am happy".

You Can & Should Yield To
The Genius Within

To be an overcomer, and avoid being defeated by challenges, in the difficult times ahead, you can Yield to the Genius Within.

It's a lifelong journey that can begin today if you choose and act. Start in the Mathew 7.7 Words of Jesus which Nick would share with you -

"Ask, and it shall be given you,
seek, and ye shall find;
knock, and it shall be opened unto you:..."

Bonus 1 –Yield to The Genius Within

1. You've The GeniusWithin–Desire to Release It
It's easiest to see as you believe in yourself. Slow down. Yield -you will wield power over your life.

2.You've Special Ability– Get Fire in Your Belly
Build a desire fire in your belly to cause it to be shown to you. Want it like a dying man.

3. Get Recognition -"Move" Internationally
Show your Ability overseas. Family don't always see your Gift. Get a partner who does.

4. You Can Clone The Genius of Your Mentor
See the Genius in your mentor. "Rub" on them. Associate with them. Read them. Live their life.

5. Get Favor with Man & God– a Servant Heart
Humble yourself and seek to be a servant to all of mankind. Begin by being a community servant.

6. You've A Million -Release It From Your Story
Your story has answers to problems people have. They'll pay to have answers now.

7. Your Thoughts Hold Gems Be a GemCollector
Collect, record, all thoughts you have. Some are gems. By collecting all & checking them out can you find the best.

You Can Make
Something Beautiful
Out of Your Life –
As You Choose
To Change Your Talk

"Your Thoughts Contain Gems –
Be A Gem Collector"

Bonus 2 –Yield to The Genius Within

1. Do ERAKS-Early Random Acts of Kindness

Give careful consideration to your Random Acts as they easily release The Genius Within.

2. Ask Permission Before Giving Advice

Only give advice to others after asking for permission to do so. Confirm their significance.

3. Mark Those That Oppose You & Avoid Them

Family-friends don't want you to change. You must.

4. You've Got Naming Rights – Use Powerfully

Get your name right. Get your product name right. And you will see The Genius released in your life.

5. Give Yourself Permission to Succeed

When you find yourself behind a barrier stopping your Genius Yield. Say, "I give myself permission"

6. Reconnect with Your Clients – Redefine Them

Redefine them as those in your care.

7. Follow the Words of Jesus -Fill The Waterpots

Make best use of things you've got. Feed your mind on your ebooks. You may fill your hands with cash.

You Can Make Something Beautiful Out of Your Life – As You Choose To Change Your Walk

"You've Got Naming Rights – Use them Powerfully"

Bonus 3 –Yield to The Genius Within

1.Get a Hand Writing Special Spot-Write Faster

As you write faster The Genius flows out. Hidden riches are in fastest writing. Control, & Improve

2. Speak Slower- Be A Toastmaster's Hero

This is a secret used by those on the speaking circuit. The Genius flows out. Audiences applaud.

3. Get to Know The Genius -Speak with Boldness

The Genius will give you a "push" inside at times. Speak boldly. Your wisdom will amaze listeners.

4.You're a Treasure NOT a Pleasure Machine

The Genius is a Treasure Machine– Please him.

5. Expect TheGenius to Spotlight Opportunities

Constantly expect opportunities .   There are no co-incidences in life. He plans and You harvest.

6. Be Prepared for the "Suddenly" Experience

Move aside & allow The Genius to do his work

7. Treat Strangers as Significant

Treat strangers as important to you and you'll both increase your significance.

You Can Make
Something Beautiful
Out Of Your Life –
As You Choose
To Change Your Thanks

"Treat Others as Significant-
&
You Get to Be Significant"

The Ultimate Challenge Eliminator

"How am I going to overcome this challenge?" You ask. Your answer can be found with the help of The GeniusWithin.

He reveals himself and gets busy eliminating challenges as you do what you were put here to do.

You have a calling to do a special task. It's the task you love the most. You may not know the task now but you can work it out.

Ask your self the Key Question - "What do you hate most?" Consider this and discover the Ultimate Challenge Eliminator.

Your answer to the Key Question will be different to others. But the outcome will be the same. Providing you ask with desire fire in your heart.

You will find your "calling" and Yield to The Genius Within who will help you as you work at the task you love the most. Your life's work will be to rid the world of that which you "hate most".

You Can Make
Something Beautiful
Out Of Your Life –
As You Choose
To Change Your Friends

"You have a "calling" to do
a special task.
It's the task you love the most."

Contact
Ken Little Can Be Contacted at his blog –

www.YieldToTheGeniusWithin.com/blog1
Click the Contact link and fill in your details.

You are encouraged to read this book three times to get the greatest blessing.

As an **Extra Bonus for Reading** This Far
You Can Go To –

www.SuccessBelongsToYou.com
and Get a Selection of
Free Resources

For the Latest on Upcoming Books
By Ken Little

You Can Follow & Friend Him at-

http://www.twitter.com/KenLittle
http://www.facebook.com/KenLittle

Where You Will Discover
Success Belongs To You